**Books are to be returned on or before
the last date below.**

LIBREX—

NEAR WATER

© Aladdin Books Ltd 1989

Designed and produced by
Aladdin Books Ltd, 70 Old Compton Street,
London W1V 5PA

Design: David West
         Children's Book Design

Illustrators: Tizzie Knowles, Aziz Khan

Pete Sanders is the head teacher of a North London
primary school and is working with teachers on
personal, social and health education.

The publishers would like to thank all the
children who posed for the pictures used in
this book.

Published in Great Britain in 1989 by
Franklin Watts Ltd, 12a Golden Square,
London W1R 4BA

ISBN 0 86313 955 8

Printed in Belgium

Introduction   4
Keeping safe   6
Safety equipment   8
Swimming   10
Staying afloat   12
On the beach   14
On a boat   16
Rain   18
Weather   20
Rivers and lakes   22
Canals and marinas   24
Thinking of others   26
Safety game   28
First Aid   30
Index   32

NEAR WATER

PETE SANDERS

GLOUCESTER PRESS

London · New York · Toronto · Sydney

Introduction

Most people enjoy playing with water, whether it's by the sea, on a river, on a lake, near a pond or maybe in a pool.

This book will help you find out about water safety. Learning this information will help you keep yourself and others safe when you are near water.

There are lots of ways in which you can enjoy yourself in and near water. You can see lots of people having fun in the picture. But not all of them are thinking about the risks of what they are doing. Can you spot what they are? Some of the dangers are listed on page 29.

Keeping safe

Playing in water is fun but you have to think about safety all the time. It doesn't seem possible but you can drown in as little as 9cm of water. To be safe you need to learn and practise water skills in a safe place. For example, you should learn to swim in a pool. It is safer here because there aren't any strong currents. Public swimming baths have attendants on duty to keep an eye on you and signs to tell you how deep the water is.

Many people join clubs to learn about sailing or canoeing. They get to know how to do things in the right way and learn how to keep out of danger.

INFORMATION

Good swimmers are not just people who can move well in the water. They've also learned the dos and don'ts of swimming. They know how important it is to test how cold the water is and they only swim in a safe place. They are aware that it is not a good idea to swim on an empty stomach or right after a meal. You should allow yourself at least two hours after eating otherwise you could get cramp.

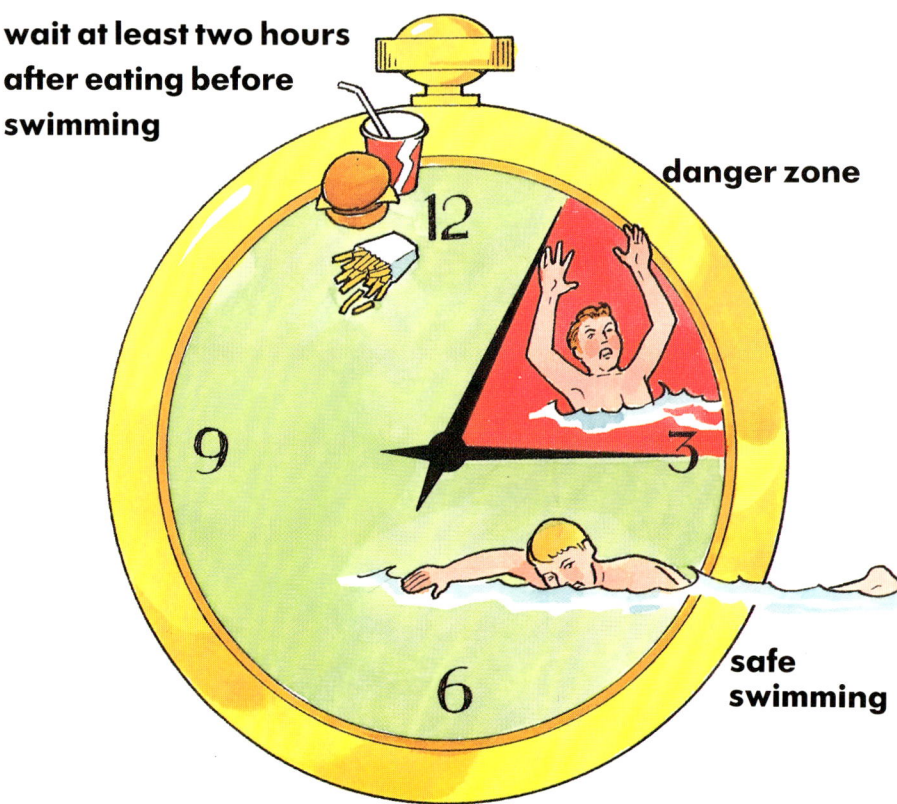

wait at least two hours after eating before swimming

danger zone

safe swimming

6

Joining a sailing club is the best way to learn about safety near water.

Safety equipment

There's a lot of equipment to keep you safe near water. People with a pond in their garden will often put a grid on top of it, particularly if there are young children about. In a swimming pool beginners wear armbands or use a float to help them swim.

On the beach there are flags to tell people about swimming conditions. People who go out to sea listen to the weather forecast. On a boat there are lifejackets, lifebuoys and anchors to keep you safe. Also available are special clothes and boots for going out to sea. For example, there are wetsuits for divers and waders for those who fish.

 **PROJECT**

Look at pages 4-5 and make a list of all the accidents that might happen. Decide which are the most common accidents and make up a sign to warn others of the risks. You might decide it's important to tell people to stay in a group when they are swimming in the sea. Another sign could show that you shouldn't swim too close to boats in case they suddenly change direction and hit you.

lifejacket and water symbol

Can you think of any others?

The rails are there to make sure you don't get too close to the pond.

When you go out in a canoe, it's important to wear a lifejacket.

Swimming

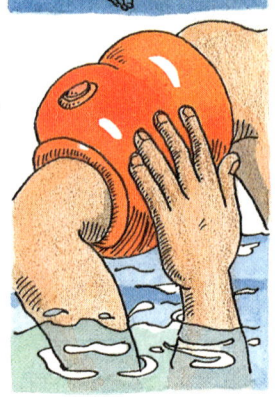

The safest place to go swimming is in a pool. But you still need to be careful. It's easy to slip on a wet surface so don't run. Think carefully about what you are doing and don't try out something unless you know you can do it. When you're learning to swim, it's best to wear inflatable arm bands.

Some people try swimming in dangerous places like water-filled gravel pits or flooded quarries. If there are steep sides they are difficult to get out of and it's not easy to judge how deep they are. You need to be especially careful with fast moving rivers or streams because you can easily be swept away.

INFORMATION

There are lots of ways of moving through water. The dog paddle means you swim like a dog with your head up, pushing the water towards you with your hands. The breast stroke is good for distance swimming and is the best one to use when you have clothes on. The back stroke is a faster style, in which you lie on your back. The crawl is the fastest way of moving through water but it is a very exhausting way to swim.

breast stroke

back stroke

crawl

You can learn how to swim if you join a class.

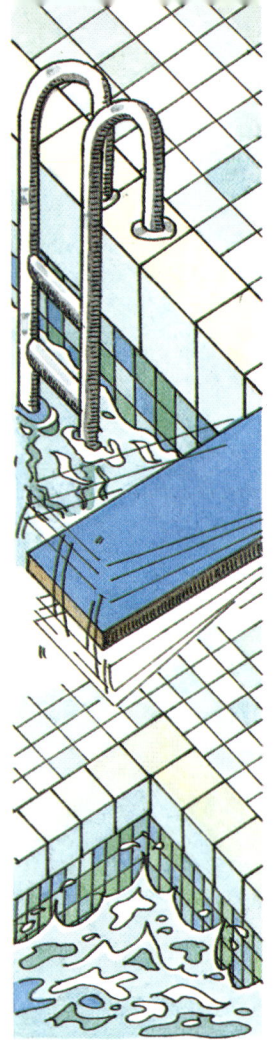

Staying afloat

When you've become good at swimming there are lots of things you need to remember to stay safe. It's not a good idea to swim in very cold water because you might get cramp. If you do get one you should stop swimming and turn on your back and float. Then you can stretch the cramped muscle by pointing your toes if the pain is in your leg.

You have to learn to judge what you can and can't do. If you find you're getting tired while out swimming, it's best to float on your back for a while. Some people use up all their energy swimming out and forget that they need to swim back.

 **INFORMATION**

Sometimes you need to have a rest while you're swimming. You can tread water by moving your arms and legs to keep you afloat. If you need help because you are exhausted and not sure whether you can swim back, signal for help. Wave one arm from side to side, keeping it straight. Use your energy for keeping afloat and don't struggle against the current because you could get overtired.

moving arms in a circular motion keeps you afloat

one arm can be used to signal and you can still tread water and keep afloat

Make sure it's deep enough before you jump into a pool.

Before swimming at the beach you need to know what the warning flags mean. A red flag means it is dangerous to swim. Flags with red on top and yellow underneath means that lifeguards are patrolling the area. Make your own designs for flags to warn people about the sea.

On the beach

Many people enjoy going to the seaside. You can go swimming, boating, windsurfing, exploring rockpools or even sunbathing. Splashing around can be a lot of fun but others may not like getting wet.

If you like swimming it's best to wade out and then swim back to the shore. Good swimmers stay close to land and swim where there is a lifeguard. If you've got a paddle boat, don't go too far out – they can sink.

You have to look out for the tides. Some people have got into trouble because they went into a cave or bay and then found themselves cut off by the tide.

PROJECT

There are two high tides a day. They happen every 12.5 hours and they change every day. The water gets even higher around the time of a new moon. You can see how much the tides vary by pushing a stick into the sand at high tide and another at low tide. You can then pace out the distance between the sticks. Try it again the next day. If you try it at a different time of the year you may find there is quite a difference.

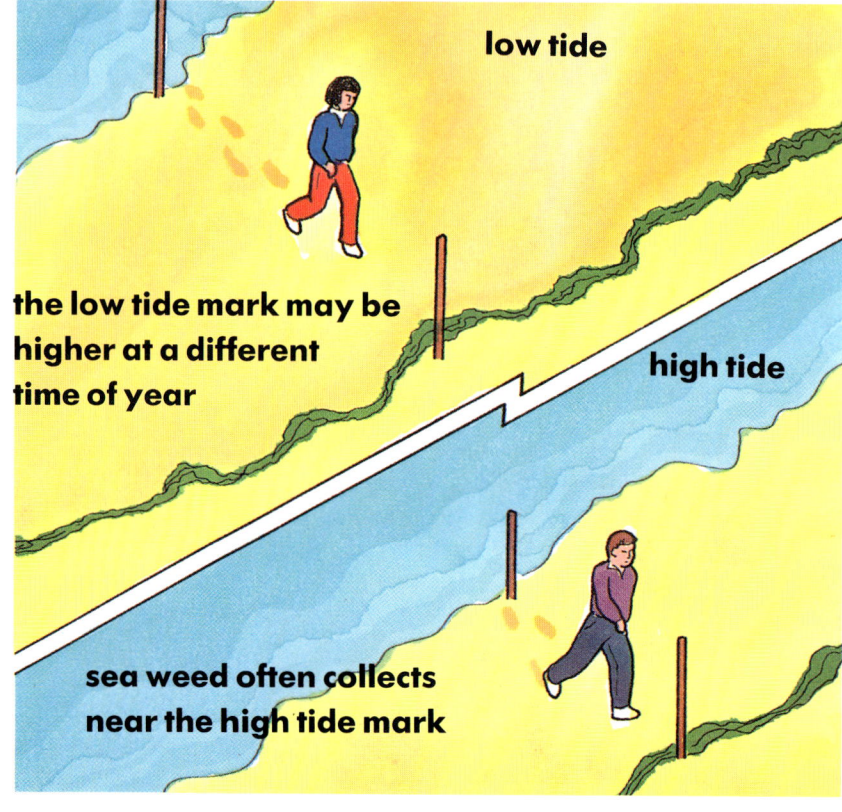

low tide

the low tide mark may be higher at a different time of year

high tide

sea weed often collects near the high tide mark

Windsurfers shouldn't get too close to swimmers.

Water moves about in the ocean in currents. The ones near the surface are caused by wind but those in the water are controlled by the tides. There is a simple way to check the current. Take an empty plastic bottle and throw it in the water. Watch which way it is being pushed.

Keep close to the shore in a paddle boat.

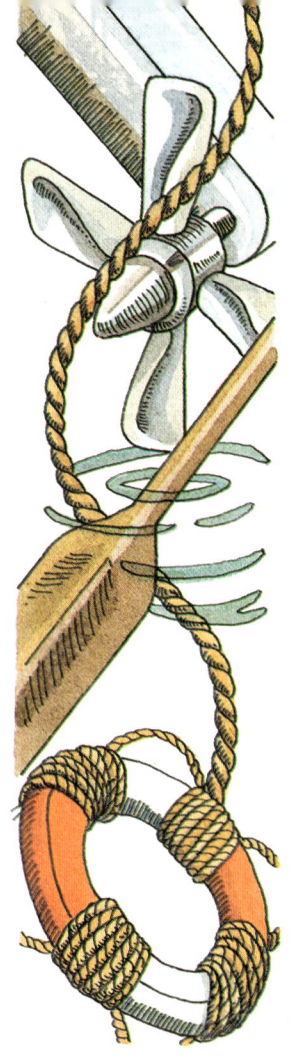

On a boat

There are many different types of boats. Some are working boats for fishing or transporting goods, others are for pleasure like sailing or canoeing. Whatever their size, shape or purpose there are rules for the people who use them. Even if you don't know all the rules, you need to remember to do what you are told in an emergency.

Anyone in charge of a boat needs to have had plenty of experience and to be able to swim. People who go canoeing have to be able to swim at least 50 metres wearing light clothing. Rowing on a pond can be fun and is safe as long as you don't do anything silly.

INFORMATION

You even have to learn how to get in and out of boats. To get into a canoe you have to place your paddle across the bank and the canoe. Then you hold onto the paddle and step into the canoe. If you're getting into a rowing boat make sure it's tied up. If it's not tied to anything it's best if an adult holds it in place while people are getting on board. Once you're in the boat don't stand up – the boat might capsize.

place paddle between bank and across the kayak

make sure the rowing boat is held

If your boat capsizes and you can't get it upright, wait for someone to help you.

Fooling around in a boat is risky.

Things that float

Collect some objects. Sort them into two piles – those you think will float and those you think will sink. Fill a bowl with water and see if you're right. An object will float if it's the right shape and weight. An empty jam jar will float because it's full of air.

Rain

Water covers more than two-thirds of the earth's surface. It's in the oceans, in rivers, lakes and even in clouds as water vapour. Rainwater usually drains into the soil. You can tell which part of a field has thick packed soil or rocks because puddles will form above it. If there are no puddles then the soil has absorbed the water. Sand absorbs water easily but clay doesn't. If you're walking in mud it's a good idea to wear Wellington boots.

Sometimes underground water is brought to the surface by digging a well. Wells can be very deep and are dangerous. You should never play near one.

INFORMATION

The water cycle

The rays from the Sun cause the water on earth to warm up and change into vapour (1). This is carried up, meets colder air and turns into tiny drops of water which join together as clouds (2). When the droplets get too large or heavy they may fall as rain (3). (If it is very cold they freeze and fall as snow, sleet or hail.) The rain runs into streams (4) which flow through rivers to the sea.

Fast flowing waters can be very strong.

Weather

When you're going near water, it's a good idea to listen to the weather forecast so you know what kind of weather to expect. You can sometimes tell that a storm is coming if the wind becomes stronger in the afternoon or evening. Another sign is if the wind changes direction suddenly.

If you're at sea you need to know the speed of the wind. It is measured on a scale of 0 when the sea is calm to 12 which is a hurricane. At 12, buildings and trees can be blown down.

Some people use a barometer to find out about the weather. It measures air pressure – a drop in pressure means a storm is likely.

 ## INFORMATION

When there's a lot of rain, floods can happen. This usually occurs near river valleys, the coast and low ground. Even a small stream can become strong enough to sweep you away. If you pitch a tent near a river, you could get very wet during a rainstorm. You have to look for ground that is higher than the river. If it's raining hard it's probably a good idea to leave the tent and find somewhere dry.

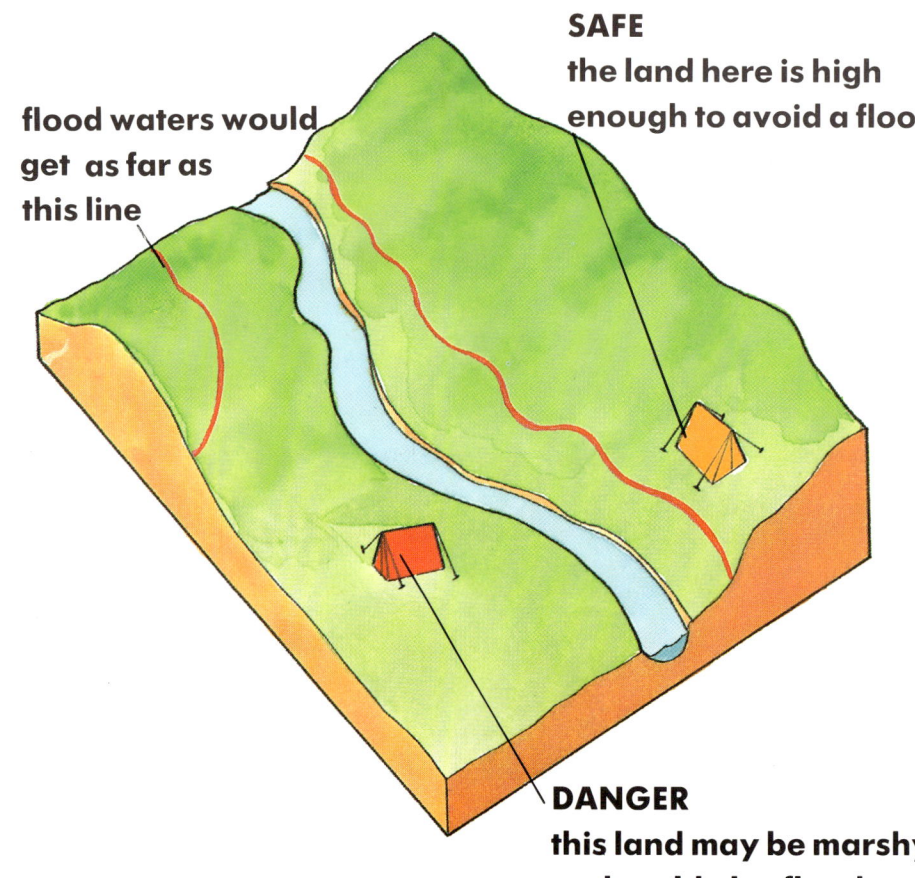

flood waters would get as far as this line

SAFE the land here is high enough to avoid a flood

DANGER this land may be marshy and could also flood

Very strong winds can bring down power lines and trees.

Setting up camp too close to water is risky.

Rivers and lakes

When rain falls on very hard ground, the water runs downhill and forms a stream. Streams join together and run into rivers. Lakes are areas of water surrounded by land. A reservoir is an artificial lake.

You have to be careful near rivers and lakes. The banks can be very slippery and people going near the water's edge can fall in. If this happens, it's best to pinch your nose and try not to swallow any water which may be polluted. Inland water can be very cold and difficult to swim in. If someone falls into a river, rescuers will help them out with a pole rather than jumping in themselves.

 ## INFORMATION

It's difficult to tell how deep a river or lake is and you can't always see what's in the water. Some swimmers get tangled in weeds. Some people cut themselves on glass or objects that have been thrown into water. Insects and bugs can cause problems. Leeches live in rivers and lakes and can attach themselves to you. You can't always tell if water is polluted. It doesn't necessarily look dirty or smell.

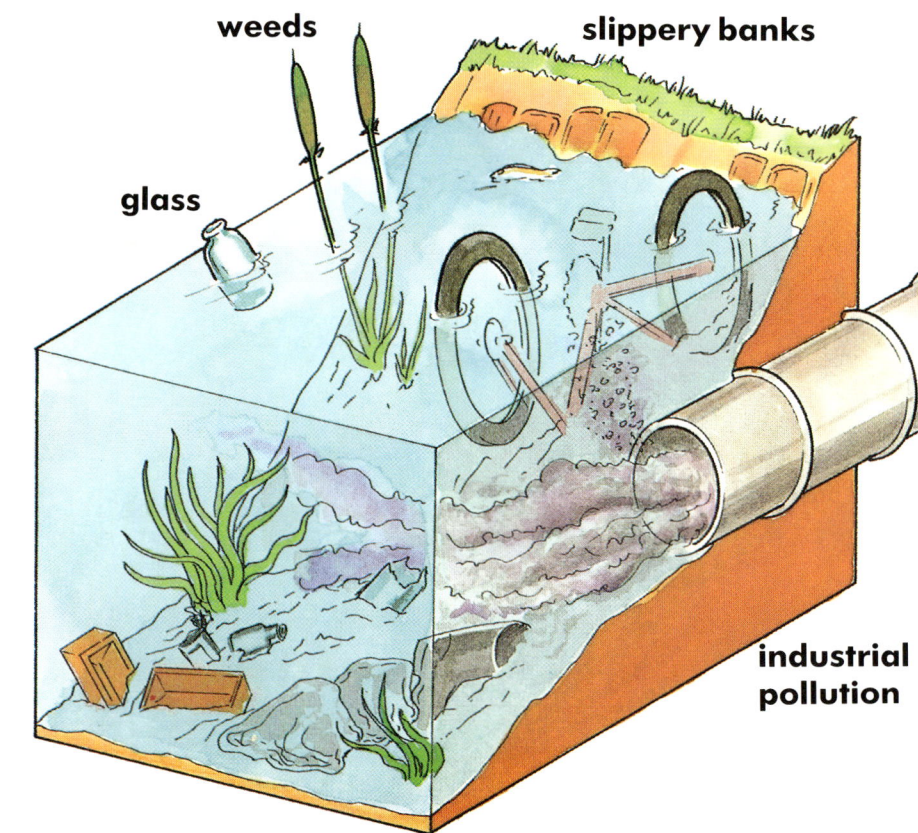

weeds

glass

slippery banks

industrial pollution

Riverbanks can be very slippery.

Keep away from rusty equipment on reservoirs.

Canals and marinas

Canals were built to transport goods cheaply a long time ago. Nowadays few of them are used for transport but many are used for boating and sightseeing. Some of them have been abandoned and are full of rubbish and stagnant water. Marinas are docks for motorboats and yachts.

Even though there are no waves or currents, canals and marinas can still be dangerous. Close to the water's edge it might be slippery. Even people walking alongside can slip and fall in. Cycling along a dock is risky. So is running. It's also worth remembering not to go alone near water.

INFORMATION

People built locks so that canals could cross hills and keep the same water level throughout. Locks have watertight gates at each end. A boat passes through a gate to get into the lock. Once both gates are closed, water is either pumped into or allowed out of the lock so that it is level with the water beyond the next lock gate. Then the lock gate is opened and the boat passes through.

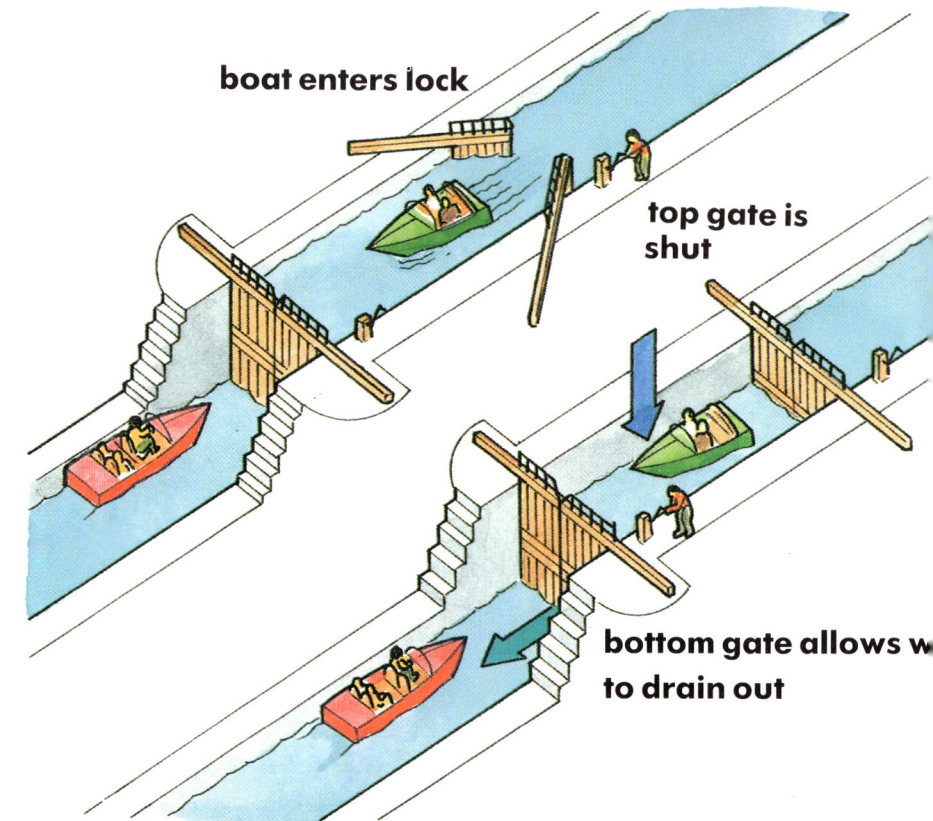

boat enters lock

top gate is shut

bottom gate allows w to drain out

It's risky leaning over the side of a canal.

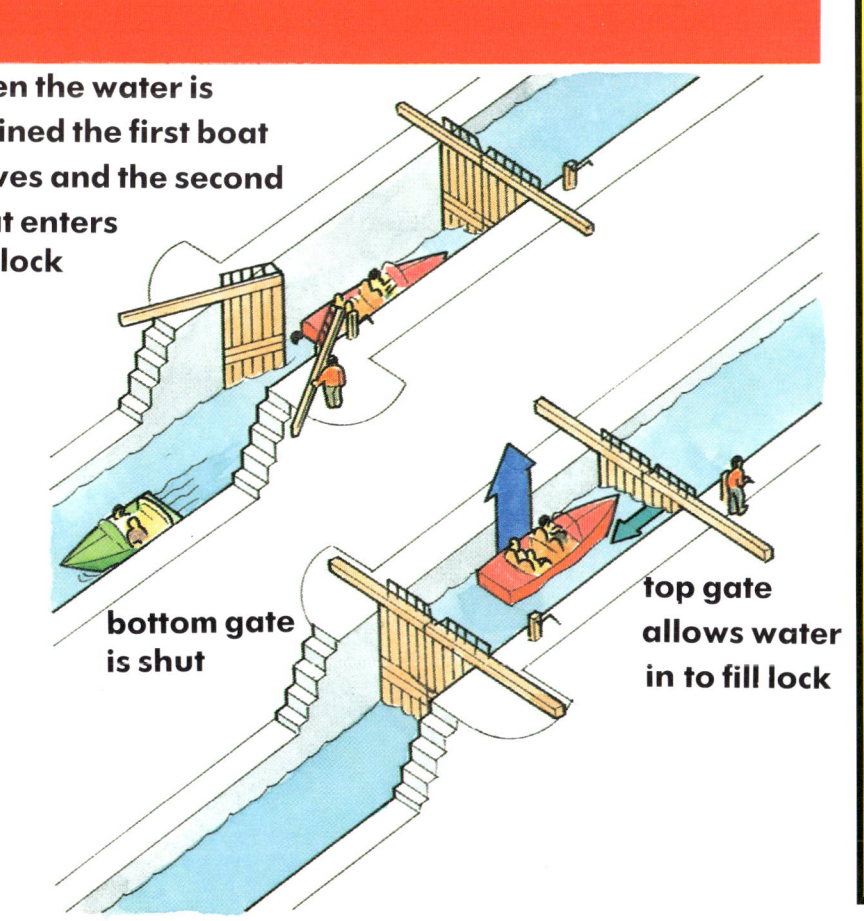

...en the water is
...ined the first boat
...ves and the second
...t enters
...lock

**bottom gate
is shut**

**top gate
allows water
in to fill lock**

The next time you go near a canal or marina make a list of all the boats you see. Write down what makes the boats move through water. For example, a barge has an engine and a canoe has paddles. Write down what each boat is being used for. Some of them may be helping people do a job.

Thinking of others

Thinking about others is important. Very young children can get frightened of waves or splashing in a paddling pool. Other people might not know enough about safety – you may need to remind a friend that going on an icy pond is dangerous because the ice could be thin and break.

It's surprising how many accidents happen because people are showing off or because they've been dared to do something. It's not a good idea to make anyone do something they're not sure of. If someone dares you to do something, you have to decide whether the risk is worth taking.

INFORMATION

Diving is only safe if you've been taught to do it properly. In a pool you have to make sure you're not going to land on someone. Wait until other swimmers are out of the way before starting to dive. Experts suggest that you should not dive into water that is less than 10 metres deep because you might hurt your head. Outdoors you also need to check that there isn't anything beneath the surface of the water.

never dive into water without knowing how deep it is

never dive when there are other swimmers

Only play on ice when an adult has told you it's thick enough.

You may need to remind your friends not to swim after eating.

Safety game

Here is a game that will help you and your friends remember safety rules near water. You can decide whether the person who wins is the one with the most counters or the one with a counter of each colour. The first player throws the die and can start wherever she or he wants to. When you land on a square with a counter, for example, canal, someone else picks up a canal card. If you answer the question correctly you get the counter. If there is no counter on the square, wait until the next turn. Everybody takes turns to have a go until someone wins.

PROJECT

Use the picture on the opposite page to draw up a board or make up your own. Use strong cardboard. Make your own figures to go round the board. You can also make your own counters. Then you need to make up lots of questions and answers to write on the cards. There are plenty of ideas in this book. Don't forget the First Aid section. You will need to look at other books to get more ideas. Make up about 20 cards for each category.

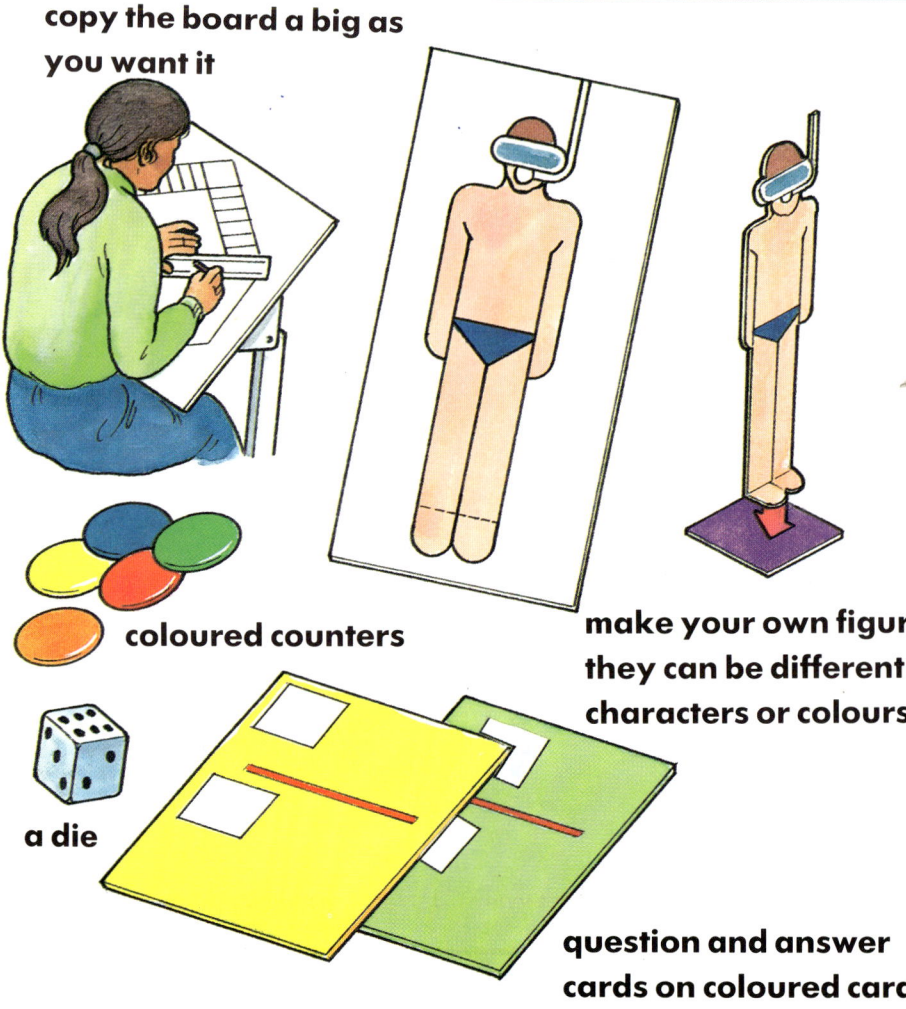

copy the board a big as you want it

coloured counters

a die

make your own figur
they can be different
characters or colours

question and answer
cards on coloured car

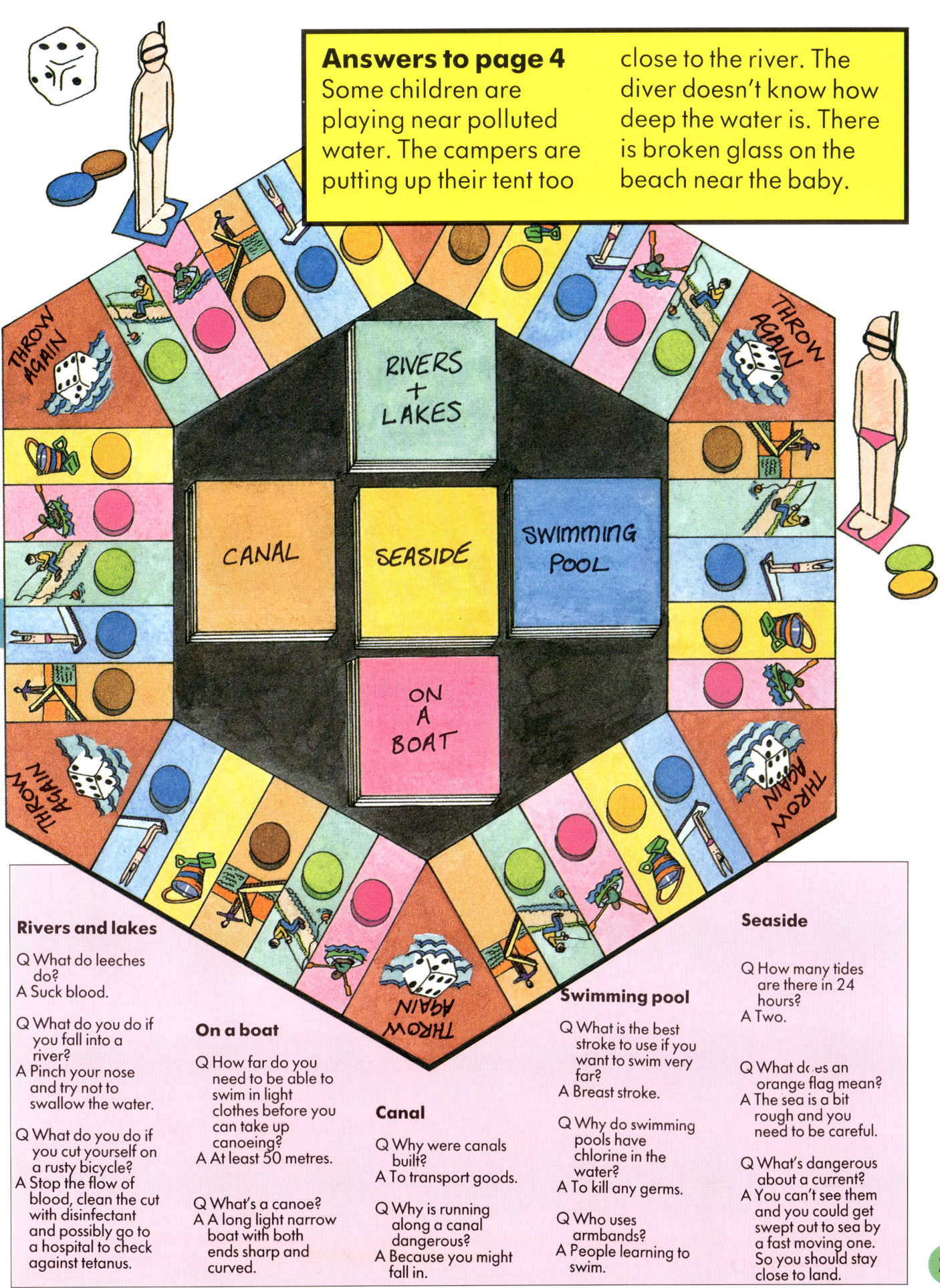

Answers to page 4
Some children are playing near polluted water. The campers are putting up their tent too close to the river. The diver doesn't know how deep the water is. There is broken glass on the beach near the baby.

RIVERS + LAKES

CANAL

SEASIDE

SWIMMING POOL

ON A BOAT

THROW AGAIN

THROW AGAIN

THROW AGAIN

THROW AGAIN

THROW AGAIN

Rivers and lakes

Q What do leeches do?
A Suck blood.

Q What do you do if you fall into a river?
A Pinch your nose and try not to swallow the water.

Q What do you do if you cut yourself on a rusty bicycle?
A Stop the flow of blood, clean the cut with disinfectant and possibly go to a hospital to check against tetanus.

On a boat

Q How far do you need to be able to swim in light clothes before you can take up canoeing?
A At least 50 metres.

Q What's a canoe?
A A long light narrow boat with both ends sharp and curved.

Canal

Q Why were canals built?
A To transport goods.

Q Why is running along a canal dangerous?
A Because you might fall in.

Swimming pool

Q What is the best stroke to use if you want to swim very far?
A Breast stroke.

Q Why do swimming pools have chlorine in the water?
A To kill any germs.

Q Who uses armbands?
A People learning to swim.

Seaside

Q How many tides are there in 24 hours?
A Two.

Q What does an orange flag mean?
A The sea is a bit rough and you need to be careful.

Q What's dangerous about a current?
A You can't see them and you could get swept out to sea by a fast moving one. So you should stay close to land.

29

First Aid

First aid is giving care and help to someone who is hurt. You need to have lessons to be good at first aid. The ideas here are to help you to know what to do if you hurt yourself or if you come across somebody who needs some help. Reading this section does not make you into an expert.

Recovery position

An injured person may look asleep. Trained first aiders check for breathing and make sure that the heart is beating. They might place the person in the recovery position. This helps the person breathe more easily and prevents choking. First you take off any glasses. You kneel about 25 centimetres away from the person and turn his or her head towards you and tilt it upwards. Then you move the arms. One is placed alongside the body and the other is bent. One leg is left straight and the other is bent.

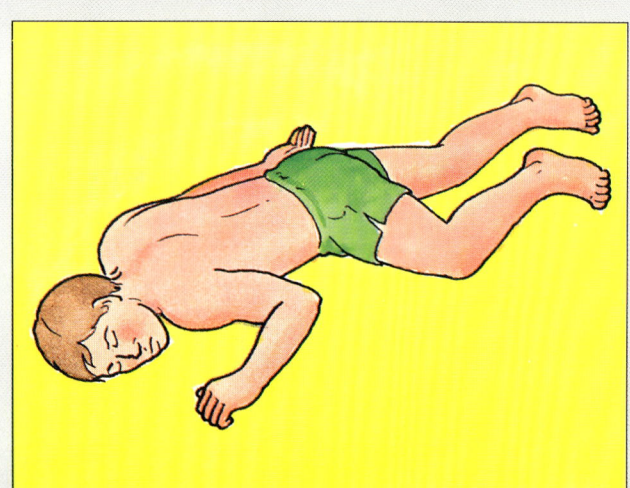

Cramp

Cramp is a sudden and painful seizing up of the muscles or group of muscles. It can happen without any warning while you are swimming. It is often caused by cold.

In the hand cramp can be helped by straightening the fingers, spreading them out and pressing on the tips. If you get cramp in the calf, straighten the leg and stand up. Press first on the heel then on the toes and keep on doing this. It's a good idea to lean forward to stretch the muscles. If you have a cramp in the thigh, you can get rid of it by sitting on the floor and straightening your leg. Another person can help here by raising your leg by the heel, and using the other

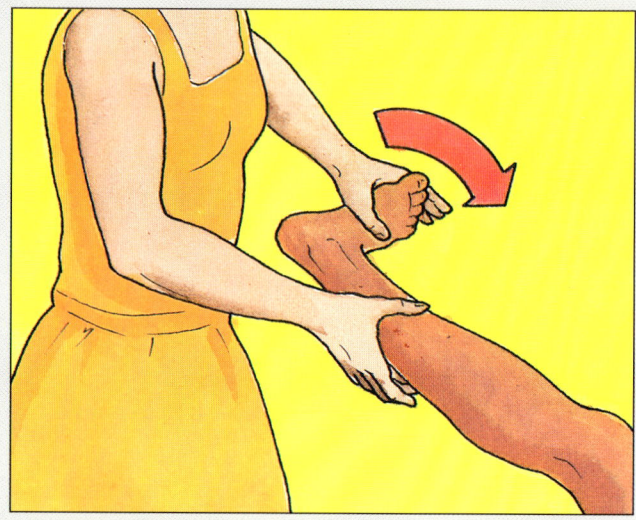

hand to press on the leg.

You can stretch the thigh muscles by bearing down on the knee. If a cramp happens in the foot, it's best to force your toes up by standing on the ball of the foot. In all cases massaging the muscles will help.

Sunburn

If you get sunburned, your skin feels hot and it can be extremely painful. You can help keep the skin cool by using calamine lotion. Or you might soak a towel in cold water and press it against the burn. Ice in plastic bag wrapped in a towel can cool the burn.

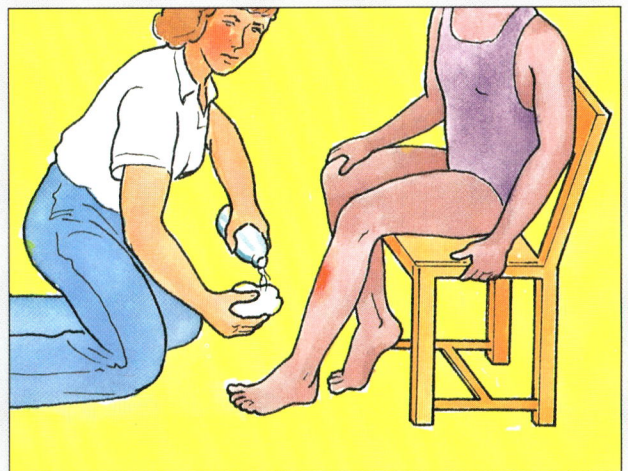

Jelly fish sting

Soak the sting in vinegar to reduce the swelling. Use disinfectant and then contact a doctor.

Hypothermia

This happens when the body's temperature drops 2 degrees lower than the normal level of 37 degrees C. If someone has hypothermia, you have to try to get them warmer. Take off any wet clothing and wrap them up in a sleeping bag or blanket. Take them to a shelter or warm room. Hot, sweet drinks will help the person get warm. Call a doctor or get the person to a hospital.

Emergency

- Keep a clear head and don't panic.
- If you see someone in distress you need to think about whether you can help or whether you need to get someone else.
- Don't put yourself in danger.
- Think of a way of getting help at once.
- If it is necessary, dial 999. The call is free.
- Know what kind of help you want – the police, the ambulance or the fire brigade.
- Be ready to give the phone number you are using, and to explain where you are.
- You will need to explain how the accident happened.
- Don't put the telephone down until the person that you are talking to has finished.

Index

beaches 8, 13, 14
boats 8, 16, 25

canals 24
cold water 12, 22
cramp 6, 12, 30
currents 6, 12, 15, 24

deep water 22, 26
diving 26
drowning 6

emergencies 31
exhaustion 12

first aid 30, 31
floating 12, 17
floods 20

hypothermia 31

jelly fish sting 31

lakes 4, 22
learning to swim 6, 10, 11
lifeguards 14
locks 24

marinas 24
mud 18

paddle boats 14, 15
polluted water 22
projects 8, 14, 17, 25, 28
public swimming baths 6

rain 18, 20, 22
recovery position 30
risks 26
rivers 4, 22
row boats 16

safety equipment 8, 10
sailing and canoeing 6, 9, 16
sailing clubs 7
storms 20
sunburn 31
swimming 6, 10, 14
swimming pools 6, 8, 10, 26

tides 14, 15
treading water 12

warning flags 13
water cycle 18
weather 8, 20
wells 18
windsurfers 15

young children 8, 26

Photographic Credits:

Cover and pages 19 and 21b: Tim and Jenny
Woodcock; pages 7, 15t and 27 both: Robert Harding
Library; page 9t: Marie-Helene Bradley; pages 9b, 11, 13,
15b, 17t, 23t and 25: Zefa; page 17b: Aladdin Pictures; page
21t: Catherine Bradley.

PRINTED IN BELGIUM BY
proost
INTERNATIONAL BOOK PRODUCTION